People's Citizenship Guide

a response to conservative canada

Funded by/Financé par

Citizenship and
Immigration Canada

Citoyenneté et
Immigration Canada

Canada

ARBEITER RING PUBLISHING · WINNIPEG

Copyright ©2011 Esyllt Jones and Adele Perry

Arbeiter Ring Publishing
201E-121 Osborne Street
Winnipeg, Manitoba
Canada R3L 1Y4
www.arbeiterring.com

Printed in Canada by Kromar Printing
Design by Relish Design Studio

With assistance of the Manitoba Arts Council/Conseil des Arts du Manitoba.

We acknowledge the support of the Canada Council for our publishing program.

ARP acknowledges the financial support to our publishing activities of the Manitoba Arts Council/Conseil des Arts du Manitoba, Manitoba Culture, Heritage and Tourism, and the Government of Canada through the Canada Book Fund.

Arbeiter Ring Publishing acknowledges the support of the Province of Manitoba through the Book Publishing Tax Credit and the Book Publisher Marketing Assistance Program.

Printed on paper with minimum 30% recycled post-consumer waste.

LIBRARY AND ARCHIVES CANADA CATALOGUING IN PUBLICATION

People's citizenship guide : a response to conservative Canada / Esyllt Jones and Adele Perry, eds.

ISBN 978-1-894037-56-3

1. Canada--History. 2. Canada--Social conditions. 3. Citizenship--Canada. 4. Immigrants--Canada. 5. Conservatism--Canada. I. Jones, Esyllt Wynne, 1964- II. Perry, Adele

FC170.P46 2011   971   C2011-907126-6

Table of Contents

Message to our Readers

NATIONS ARE COMPLICATED *and so are our feelings about them. Canada has a long history of repression, exclusion, and exploitation. But Canada is also a diverse country made of the labour, ideas, and cultures we all contribute.*

Canada is built on Indigenous land. For 400 years, non-Indigenous people—first French, then English, then Canadian—have claimed it. Some newcomers to Canada have been welcomed and respected, while others have been banned, marginalized, and made to feel unwelcome. And Canada is still a colonial society. It is a "constitutional monarchy" with images of the British Queen on its money—and recently reinstalled in government offices abroad.

Immigrants arriving at Winnipeg Station, ca. 1909

The Canadian government requires a long list of things from people who are applying for citizenship, including a test of their knowledge of Canada. But much of the "Canada" on which this test is based reflects a nationalistic, militaristic, and racist view of Canada and its history.

This guide is about a different kind of Canadian identity, one you won't find in the official version. Canadians have long questioned what Canada is and what it can and should be. Indigenous people have resisted the Canadian state, French Canadians have articulated their own version of Canada, and women, workers, and immigrants have all fought to make Canada more just and more equitable.

Although we believe this guide gives a more accurate and honest account of Canada, we do not suggest it is the one "correct" version. It was written by a group of people from particular backgrounds, with differing perspectives, with more knowledge about some things and less about others. Unlike the Canadian government, we do not wish to enforce a monolithic view of Canada that excludes whatever facts and experiences complicate its nostalgia for a simple past that never really was. Above all, this guide is meant to challenge the current government's approach, and instead encourage everyone to question what it means to be a citizen of Canada.

Just to be clear, this guide will not help anyone pass the test to really become a citizen of Canada. For that, you should visit the website of Citizenship and Immigration Canada at <www.cic.bc.ca.>

Oaths, Citizenships, and Canadas

When people become Canadian citizens, they are required to repeat a string of peculiar, old-fashioned words and make some pretty sweeping promises to the British Monarch, Canadian laws, and to something called the "duties of Canadian citizenship." Canada's federal government has recently made the role of the military much more prominent in citizenship ceremonies. The government believes that a military official should be present at the ceremony, seated near the citizenship judge. As of October 2011, a high-ranking member of the military may preside over citizenship ceremonies, entirely replacing the citizenship judge. One of the military official's tasks will be to speak to new citizens about the "responsibilities and privileges of Canadian citizenship." These are symbolic changes—which does not mean they are not important. They reflect the current government's attempt to create a more militarized Canadian society, even as much as it embraces the economic and social agenda of the new right.

The authors who produced this guide do not share this government's vision of what Canada was, is, or might become. We want a Canada that offers a more equitable kind of citizenship. Some of us question whether there should be national borders and laws that make some people citizens and others not. We all question the kind of Canada that Stephen Harper and his government are advancing.

The Politics of Citizenship

Citizens have the right to make key demands on and receive benefits from the government. For much of Canadian history, people were French or British subjects rather than citizens of a nation. The *Citizenship Act* of 1947 created the legal category of Canadian citizenship and repealed bluntly racist aspects of Canada's immigration policy. But citizenship was not and would not be available to all. Canada's immigration policies explicitly favoured people from Europe until the 1960s, and continue to function in ways that privilege people with money and certain kinds of training and skills. More and more people fall outside of the protections of citizenship. There are perhaps half a million undocumented workers in Canada. There are hundreds of thousands of people, many of them domestic or agricultural workers from the Global South, who enter Canada under federal programs that deny them the basic rights of citizens.

The Rights of Citizenship

Canadian politicians today speak of human rights as individual civil and political rights combined with citizens' responsibilities to the state. In practice, Canada's history reveals a culture of rights that embraces collective rights; social, economic and cultural rights; and citizens' duty to their community.

Human rights are recognized in Canadian law through Acts of Parliament and the provincial legislatures; English Common Law; and French Civil Law. For many years Canadian governments refused to recognize international law. Canada even voted initially against the Universal Declaration of Human Rights. Despite state opposition, social movements and Canada's legal community have sought out international law as a source of inspiration and guidance for human rights.

Fundamental Freedoms

When British settlers conquered British North America they brought with them a tradition of individual rights that was first enshrined in law under the *Magna Carta* in 1215. The *British North America Act* (1867) recognized the rights of Catholics and Protestants but excluded Aboriginal peoples, and soon after the *Indian Act* denied even the most basic rights to Aboriginals. The most fundamental rights of citizenship, including the right to vote or serve in public office, were denied to women and most minorities, in some cases until the mid-twentieth century. Anti-discrimination laws were introduced across Canada by 1977, and in 1982 human rights were embedded in the constitution through the *Charter of Rights and Freedoms*.

Settlers enjoyed certain fundamental freedoms, and these freedoms have only recently been enjoyed equally among Canadian citizens: Freedom of conscience and religion; Freedom of thought, belief, opinion and expression, including freedom of speech and of the press; Freedom of peaceful assembly; and Freedom of association. *Habeas corpus*, the right to challenge unlawful detention by the state, as well as due process in law, is also fundamental to human rights. These rights are continually threatened. The Canadian state has used fears surrounding terrorism to suspend human rights.

An informed and engaged citizenry is the best protection against state abuse of powers. The *Charter of Rights and Freedoms*, as well as federal and provincial human rights statutes, guarantee to each citizen basic human rights. The most important of these rights include:

Life, Liberty and Security of the Person: Bodily integrity and personal security are protected from state interference that violates "principles of fundamental justice." This section of the Charter has been used to protect the right to due process. In criminal investigations and trials, the prosecution must disclose to the accused person the case against them. The courts have ruled that refugee claimants cannot be deported if they face imminent threats upon return. Criminals cannot be extradited if they face the death penalty.

Mobility Rights: Canadians can live and work anywhere in Canada, enter and leave the country freely, and apply for a passport. Canadian citizens should not be deported or have their citizenship revoked.

Equality Rights: Canadians have the right not to be discriminated against and the right to reasonable accommodation from employers, landlords and service providers. This includes, among others, sexual orientation, disability, race, ethnicity, religion, gender and age.

Aboriginal Peoples' Rights: The rights guaranteed in the Charter are not to adversely affect any treaty or other rights and freedoms of Aboriginal peoples. Aboriginal people claim the right to self-government, control over their ancient lands, and to retain their culture and identity.

Official Language Rights and Minority Language Education Rights: French and English have equal status in Parliament and throughout the federal government. Language rights are a fundamental freedom in Canada. Canadian citizens have the right to be educated in English or French irrespective of where they live in Canada.

Multiculturalism: Most Canadians embrace multiculturalism as a fundamental Canadian value, although it is often poorly recognized in state policy. Too often governments seek to promote a "thin" multiculturalism and fail to address the social and economic marginalization of new Canadians.

Social, economic, and cultural rights are also fundamental human rights. Canadian citizens have the right to: organize and join a trade union; proper medical care, including abortions or prescription drugs; affordable education; privacy, especially from the state and corporations; and social assistance in the case of unemployment, poor health, or old age. Every Canadian has the right to work and be educated. In Quebec, French is the official language, and French Canadians have the collective right to maintain their language and culture.

In Canada, men and women are equal under the law. Canadian law also recognizes that women were denied equal rights in the past and continue to face inequality in the workplace and in society. Many institutions in Canada have equity policies to ensure equal access for women. These policies do not privilege women; they acknowledge and address past and present inequalities.

Who We Are

L ike all nations, Canada is a construct, a product of collective imagination and history.

Aboriginal Peoples

For many First Nations, the nation-state of Canada is an imposition, and often an unwelcome one. Indigenous people have lived in the territories now called Canada for tens of thousands of years. Since the Canadian state has existed, it has been at best ambivalent and at worst explicitly hostile to First Nations, determined to challenge Indigenous peoples and their claims to the land and its resources.

Canada is built on First Nations land and its wealth is derived from the resources contained within it. Many First Nations never surrendered these lands or these resources. The reserves that were laid out to keep First Nations contained so that they would not disrupt this exploitation are hopelessly small, fragments of those traditional territories that sustained the people. The Canadian state defined them as "Indians" and enacted laws that governed choices of marriage, where they could live, prohibiting from them the right to own land, to vote and to enter the professions. West of the

Wampum

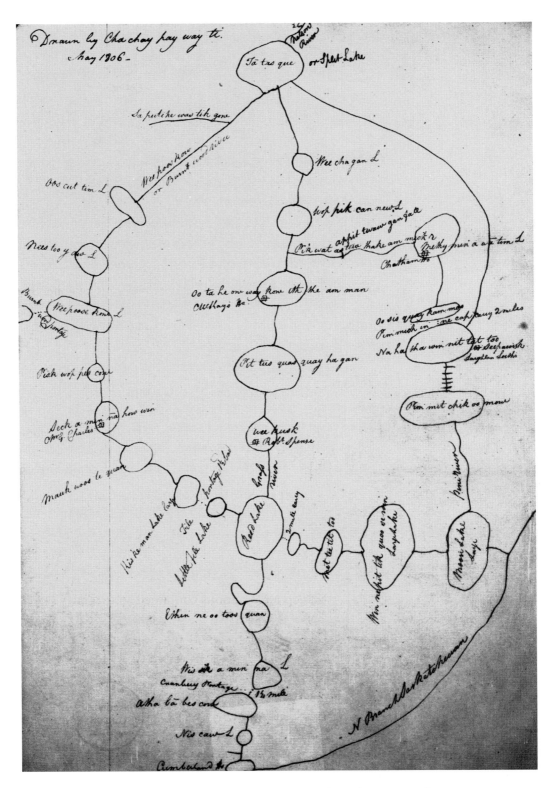

Cha Chay Pay Way Ti's Map of the Waterways of a Part of Northern Manitoba, 1806

Great Lakes, people of European and Aboriginal descent formed their own Métis society. Twice the Canadian government sent the army to oppose them. In the twentieth century, the government forcibly moved Inuit peoples off their land and into villages, sometimes much farther north than they had lived in centuries, where many starved. Today, the Inuit have jurisdictional control over their own territory, Nunavut, and they are working to heal the harms done by Canada. It is with considerable irony that First Nations reflect on the line in our national anthem, "O Canada: our home and native land." Whose land is it, and at what costs?

Settlers

Since the 1600s, newcomers have come to settle permanently in Canada. For working people from France and later Britain, a move to Canada might mean greater economic stability, though it could put them into direct conflict with First Nations people who knew the land to be theirs.

Many settlers came to farm but found no cheap land and instead worked for wages in the industrial economy that emerged in the 1800s. They built canals or railways, found work in isolated lumber camps and mines or on the factory floors of Montreal and Toronto. Different settler groups have been accorded different resources, rights, and respect. People came from China, even if they had to pay a tax to enter the country from 1885 to 1923, and were excluded from doing so between 1923 and 1947. Japanese and South Asian families negotiated an exclusionary immigration policy in order to migrate and they built successful fishing fleets, farms and sawmills despite the poor welcome they received.

Canada's History

When Indigenous people encountered settlers, they did so with the knowledge and experience of dealing with different nations. Nearly 100 languages were spoken in the territories that predated Canada. First Nations had distinct territories, but also extensive relations and sometimes conflicts with neighbouring nations, and were alert to new opportunities and ideas. These histories and resources would be used and tested when Europeans began to explore, trade, work, and then settle in Indigneous territories.

Portrait of a Haitian woman, François Maléport de Beaucourt, 1786

At the end of the 1600s, wealthy Europeans began to see northern North America as a potential source of wealth, power and prestige. But it was working people, mainly fishers and sealers, from Normandy, Brittany, and the Basque country, who first spent any time in Canada. These men spent most of their summers ashore where they attracted the attention of Mi'kmaq, Maliseet, and Abenaki peoples. Europeans soon learned that First Nations were avid traders willing to trade valuable animal furs for the trade goods Europeans brought, especially metal goods. This small-scale trade provided the basis for Canada's place in an emerging world economy.

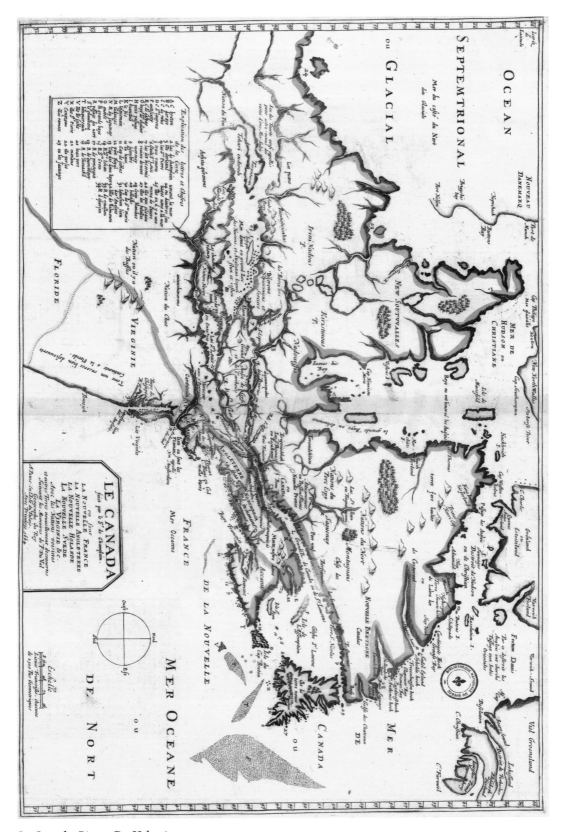

Le Canada, Pierre Du Val, 1653

Enmeshed in Empire

Few today think of Canada as a place born of empire. But its early history is one of empire, and the legacies of this history haunt us still. The wealthy of Europe looked to the "new world" for wealth and prestige, but were often compelled to turn to private companies or individuals to administer their interests and ambitions. Samuel de Champlain, famed explorer of New France, was one of these. He brought the first settlers to New France in 1608–09, but when a mutiny and then scurvy killed off more than half the inhabitants in the first year, investors withdrew their support. At first, the British also let business take care of colony building. In 1670, the Hudson's

The Pallisaded Village of Lachine 1689, **Walter Baker**

Encampment of the Loyalists in Johnstown, a new settlement on the banks of the River St. Lawrence, in Canada West, J.R. Simpson James Peachy (after), 1925.

Bay Company was granted most of the continent's interior as a fur-trading monopoly. It succeeded because it worked with Aboriginal networks of trade and labour. But Canada did not live up to the visions of entrepreneurs who dreamed of quick and easy profits. Leaving the building of Canada in the hands of business was risky.

Chaos and War

The history of Canada's early colonies is one of warfare and chaos. European firepower was introduced in the seventeenth century, making warfare much more deadly. To the east of the Great Lakes, First Nations fought in alliance with different European powers, and against other First Nations. Epidemic disease intensified the social dislocations of war. In 1634–35, a smallpox epidemic compounded the conflict between the Hauenausaune and the Wendat and their allies, and the latter were decimated and reduced to refugee communities scattered along the Great Lakes and up the St. Lawrence.

In 1663, New France was established as a colony of France. France sent thousands of soldiers to protect the colony and sponsored the immigration of women called *filles du roi*. Many Quebecois today trace their genealogies to these first settlers. New France was an agricultural society, organized around the seigneurial system, a hierarchical and semi-feudal system that put peasants or habitants under the authority of landowners. It was also a slave-holding society. Enslaved people of both African and Indigenous origin were concentrated in domestic work, and owning a slave in New France could be an important status symbol for the colony's elite.

The royal takeover of New France did not bring peace to the region. The century between the late 1600s and the late 1700s was one of nearly constant war between France and England, fought in part on North American ground with Aboriginal allies. For both soliders and civilians, this was a war of torture, captivity, and the destruction of homes, crops, and communities. The *Treaty of Utrecht* formally ended hostilities in 1713, but small-scale raids continued in the 1720s. War broke out again in the 1740s and continued despite further peace treaties. In 1713, the French ceded part of Acadia—a prosperous agricultural colony in what today is Atlantic Canada—to Britain. Between 1755 and 1759, over 10,000 largely French-speaking, Roman Catholic Acadians were forcibly removed from their homes. Then they were then transported to British colonies to the south, where they lived as unwanted and dispossessed refugees. Like the First Nations, the Acadians paid dearly for Canada's role in the global politics of empire.

With the conquest of Quebec, England took control of French Canada in 1760. Britain struggled to administer a colony populated by largely French-speaking, Roman Catholic settlers. Early efforts at blunt assimilation failed, and Britain was forced to find ways to accommodate French Canada. In 1774 the *Quebec Act* was passed, allowing the use of French civil law, and offering Catholics the right to practice their religion and hold public office. But it did not permit an elected assembly.

Objections to this kind of government informed the American Revolution, which broke out two years later. Canada was again plunged into violence. Age-old relationships were torn apart as Aboriginal nations chose sides. Americans twice attempted to invade. Privateers disrupted trade, and there were severe food shortages on the east coast. When the American Revolution succeeded, those who stayed loyal to Britain became refugees, forced to leave their homes and property and travel north to what became Canada.

Ineffective Government, Repressive Regimes and Alternative Visions

By the early 1800s, a new vision of a British Canada had emerged, one rooted in claims of its distinctiveness from the republican, slave-holding society to the south. Slavery had been practiced in both French and English colonies. Upper Canada began to gradually disallow slavery in 1793, though it was not until slavery was abolished in the British Empire in 1834 that it was actually illegal. It was after this that Canada became a refuge for African Americans fleeing the violence and exploitation of slavery. The segregated schools,

The Burning of the Parliament Building in Montreal, ca. 1849

isolated communities, and limited job prospects that they found in Canada made clear that racism remained even where slavery did not.

The notion of Canada's distinctiveness also justified a very limited sort of democracy and self-government. In British colonies, the upper levels of government were appointed, not elected. Adults with property could vote for the elected assembly, and Newfoundland didn't have that

until 1832. Some women with property could vote, until they were disenfranchised in 1849. Everywhere in British North America, politics was largely for the well-resourced. Those who were elected to the assembly were not paid, so only the well-off could run for election. The legislative council and the appointed governor could veto any legislation passed by the elected assembly that it did not like. Men appointed to the legislative council used their positions to increase their own wealth.

Back view of the church of St. Eustache and dispersion of the insurgents, Lord Charles Beauclerk, 1840

In 1837 and 1838, people in both English and French Canada responded with armed rebellion. In Lower Canada (what is now Quebec), the rebels led by Louis Joseph Papineau offered an alternative vision of a democratic, republican and French-speaking Canada. The British colonial government responded with a devastating crackdown. Whole towns in Quebec were burned as punishment and captured rebels were hanged or transported against their will to Australia. Lord Durham, sent to investigate the situation, blamed French Canadians for much of the unrest. The British forced together Upper and Lower Canada under one government with two provinces, hoping that French interests and culture would drown in a sea of English institutions and settlement. But

Durham also recommended that the government's leaders be elected and responsible to the elected assembly, not to the British governor. Democracy was a step closer but far from fully achieved.

Who Built Canada?

In this environment of conflict, exploitation, and war, it was ordinary people, Indigenous and settler, women and men, who built Canada. Poor young widows like Francoise Brunet who came to New France as a *fille du roi* in 1663. Leaders like the Seneca chief Tekanoet who traveled to Montreal in 1701 to negotiate a lasting peace. Men like Samuel Lount, who lost his life in the pursuit of democracy in the 1837–38 rebellions. Chloe Cooley, the enslaved woman whose protest set into motion changes that would end with the banning of slavery in Upper Canada. The countless contributions of working people, living lives in keeping with their own vision of Canada, built this country just as surely as its political leaders.

Notice to Intending Emigrants for North America. For Sydney, Cape Briton, Pictou, Nova Scotia & Quebec, July 15, 1845

From Colony to Colonizer: Confederation

In 1867, a collection of colonies became a nation. New Brunswick, Nova Scotia, Canada West and Canada East came together to form the self-governing "dominion" of Canada. Confederation was not the result of a great upsurge of patriotic feeling. Indeed, many "fathers" of confederation had urged joining the United States only a few years before. Nova Scotia's and Prince Edward Island's leaders were deeply divided, and Newfoundland stayed out until 1949. British Columbia's settlers, who made up only a small portion of the territory's population, were split between those who wished to join the U.S., those who wished to remain a British colony, and those who wished to join Canada.

Interior of workshop, John Henry Walker, 1850–1885

Louis Riel,
Montreal, Quebec,
1868

Confederation marked the end of Canada's history as a British colony, but the beginning of its career as a colonizing force. New laws defined who was and who was not an "Indian" and curtailed the rights of those who were. Women who married "non-Indians" became non-Indian and had to leave their homes and communities. With an eye to freeing up western lands occupied by Métis and First Nations, the federal government negotiated the first of the numbered treaties and began to pursue policies of reserve settlement and residential schooling.

The majority of people living in the lands that would become Canada had no input at all into the government and laws of this new country. There was no vote on Confederation, and even if there had been, most people living in Canada had no voting rights. Women, those under 21, and those without property had no formal political say. Immigrants could only vote if they came from somewhere else in the British Empire, and First Nations were almost always denied the right to vote, as were Asian Canadians on the West Coast.

The First Nations and Métis people of what is now Manitoba, Saskatchewan and Alberta would feel the sharp power of the new nation. In 1869, Canada bought the territory from the Hudson's Bay Company, in what amounted to a real estate transaction. The Métis, led by Louis Riel, denounced this plan and created their own government to negotiate the same guarantees and rights that other regions had been given, and recognition of Métis land-holding, language, and religion. They won a significant portion of these rights, but Canada failed to deliver on some critical promises.

Home of Galician
settlers, Rosthern,
Saskatchewan,
about 1910

Native graveyard, Lebret,
Saskatchewan, 1885

Many Métis never received the land promised to them in Manitoba. In 1885, again represented by Riel, they fought to protect their rights as they had fifteen years earlier. This time Prime Minister John A. Macdonald did not negotiate. He used the Canadian army to crush the resistance with artillery, machine guns, and infantry, the tactics perfected by the British in their many "small wars" of empire around the globe. Louis Riel and eight First Nations leaders were hanged, and others were imprisoned.

This marked the beginning of a terrible stretch of years for western Aboriginal peoples. They were forced onto too-small reserves, given too little aid, their children were placed in residential schools, and their cherished spiritual ceremonies were banned.

Inequality was woven into the fabric of the new nation. Married women could not own property or control their own wages. Women could not vote in federal elections until 1918. People from China, Japan, India, and African Americans were all subject to legal and extra-legal means of keeping Canada white. Chinese, Indo, and Japanese Canadians were denied the right to vote until 1947, as were First Nations people until 1960.

The idea of a "white" Canada came in handy for industrial capitalism. Canada's empire builders wanted cheap labour. Often with the support of government, they tried to keep wages down by keeping unions weak or out of the workplace completely. Employers used technology to shrink the work force, deported "trouble-makers," and opposed stronger labour laws such as minimum wages, shorter work days, and safety regulations. Employers benefited from racism among "white" Canadians. This allowed them to pit workers against one another and divide them by race. Sexism made the same thing

possible, creating a lack of solidarity between male and female workers. Women were often paid less than half of what men earned.

Mothers' Picnic, Stanley Park, Vancouver, 1935

Women and men did fight for better conditions. Many were arrested, imprisoned, deported, and some were murdered. Workers formed unions and went on strike. A few examples are the Nova Scotia miners' strike of 1909–10, the Winnipeg General Strike of 1919, the On-to-Ottawa Trek against unemployment in 1935, and the Windsor auto strike of 1945.

Laws limiting the number of hours workers could be made to labour and setting minimum wages were a response to labour's activism. Legislation providing incomes for elderly people or lone

Presentation of petition by Political Equality League for enfranchisement of women, Winnipeg, December 23, 1915

mothers was a response to those who argued that the federal and provincial governments had a responsibility to the poor. People built social movements that demanded a more meaningful democracy. Free speech advocates risked arrest to win the right to gather and speak out publicly. Women won the right to vote with rallies, demonstrations, lobbying, court cases and civil disobedience.

Migrants challenged discriminatory policies. In 1908, the government insisted that would-be immigrants make the voyage from their homeland to Canada in a single, continuous voyage. This was a thinly veiled attempt to stop immigration from India. In 1914, about 375 Indian Sikhs, Hindus, and Muslims fought the Continuous Passage law by chartering a ship, the *Komagata Maru*, to take them from Hong Kong to Vancouver. The government refused to let the ship dock and confined the passengers to the ship for several weeks. They were forced to return to India.

War and Civil Rights

Then as now war exposes racism and xenophobia. Canada violated the rights of its people during both World Wars. During World War I (1914–1918), Canadians from Germany and the Austro-Hungarian Empire were held in internment camps. Even Canadian birth didn't

protect people of Japanese origin during World War II (1939–1945). Japanese-Canadians were placed in internment and forced labour camps, and their belongings and homes were sold. They remained in those camps until the war was over, then thousands were deported to Japan—a country many of them had never seen. Numerous Japanese-Canadians never returned to their homes in British Columbia.

The Komagata Maru in Vancouver's Port, July 1914

Some of the first Cree enlistees, The Pas, Manitoba, 1914

Internment camp
at Banff, Alberta,
ca. 1914–18

Waving goodbye to
Japanese Canadians
being sent to a
work camp near
Jasper, Alberta in
February 1942

Modern Canada

Many forces shaped Canada in the aftermath of the Second World War: economic growth and the Cold War; global decolonization and Aboriginal resistance; nationalism, and regionalism. Social movements—demanding women's and workers' rights, an end to racism, war, and environmental degradation—helped shape a changing postwar world.

Signs from a protest against Canada's involvement in global wars.

Trade and Economic Growth

The Canadian economy forms part of an unequal global economic system, a system which, shaped by the legacies of colonialism, continues to privilege industrialized nations over those of the global south. The postwar period was a time of economic boom for wealthy nations like Canada, and many Canadians achieved greater material comfort than they had previously enjoyed. This economic growth, however, was not equally shared. Men earned more than women, and those who spoke English earned more than those who spoke French. Aboriginal Canadians and racial minorities were the least advantaged of all.

It was also in the postwar period that Canada was drawn into the Cold War, during which capitalist Western nations allied themselves with the United States in opposition to the communist Soviet Union. The Cold War affected Canada in many ways. Fear of communism meant that healthy dissent was suppressed. Social conformity was emphasized. Gays and lesbians, especially those in the federal civil service and the military, were unfairly persecuted, which ruined many lives and careers. Their ingeneous ways of resisting the conformity of the era paved the way for future dissident movements.

International Roles

Members of the Akwesasne Mohawk Warrior Society reclaim Loon Island, near Cornwall, Ontario, 1970

In the years following World War II, many former colonies achieved independence, although decolonization often led to new forms of subjugation to either the United States or the Soviet Union. Canada supported the creation of the United Nations, and many Canadians worked for peace and against nuclear weapons. However, Canada remained an important member of the North Atlantic Treaty Organization. Through this military alliance, the country promoted the interests of its Western allies over the needs of the decolonizing world. Canada supplied arms to the French government as it fought with those hoping to achieve independence in North Africa. Canadian industry manufactured weapons used by the United States during the Vietnam War. The American military even tested Agent Orange at a military base in New Brunswick. Canada helped destabilize Jean-Bertrand Aristide's elected government of

Haiti, which was deposed by a coup in 2004. And since 2001, Canada has been involved in the Afghanistan war, making it an ally of the United States in the Middle East.

Anti-war protest, Calgary, 1972

While Canada claimed to bring democracy to distant lands, Aboriginal peoples have consistently reminded Canadians of the legacies and present day realities of colonialism. Suffering much higher rates of suicide and diseases such as diabetes than the Canadian average, for Aboriginal peoples the effects of racism and discrimination have not gone away.

A Modern Society

Since the 1950s, Canada has certainly made some progress towards racial and sexual equality. Social programs such as Medicare, income assistance, and public pensions have provided some economic security to individuals and families. These changes did not happen on their own. They were the product of hard-fought struggles by social movements and their political allies. In the 1960s and 1970s women formed a variety of feminist organizations that demanded the right to birth control, abortion, equal pay for equal work, childcare, and more. The modern environmental movement was born, raising awareness of the often destructive impact of human activity on the natural world. The movement for gay and lesbian rights emerged. Workers finally won the legal right to form unions and bargain collectively with their employers. They used this right to demand increased wages, democracy in the workplace, and individual and collective security. For a time, class inequality lessened in Canada. Black Canadians demanded an end to racism and the promotion of social justice, both at home and abroad. Some of these movements argued that social justice could only be achieved through a complete restructuring of society. Others fought for concrete reforms and changes in the existing system.

New Canadians learning English, Calgary, Alberta, February 1977

In the postwar period large numbers of newcomers arrived in the country. Because immigration regulations discriminated on the basis of race, the vast majority of immigrants were white, mostly from Europe. Anti-Semitism, political bias, and discrimination against homosexuals also shaped immigration policies. In the 1960s, Canada removed the most overtly racist aspects of its immigration laws. Many discriminatory aspects remained. There were more Canadian immigration offices in wealthy nations than poor ones. Certain employment skills were valued over others. These policies made it easier to exclude working people from the global south.

During the Cold War, Canada opened its doors to many refugees. It accepted tens of thousands from Hungary after the 1956 uprising, and thousands from Czechoslovakia after the Prague Spring of 1968. The Canadian government welcomed those fleeing

North End Winnipeg,
Manitoba, ca. 1979

communist dictatorships. This response was not matched by its treatment of refugees from right-wing dictatorships. Canada was slow and inflexible in its response to the refugee crisis created by the CIA-backed coup in Chile in 1973. Throughout the 1970s Canada deported many Haitians, sending them back to live under the dictatorship of Jean-Claude Duvalier.

Some of the largest changes that took place in postwar Canada occurred in Quebec. In the aftermath of the war and through the 1950s, Quebec politics were dominated by Maurice Duplessis. As provincial premier, he was strongly supported by the Roman Catholic Church and big business. But Quebec was not somehow backwards or static. Brewing discontent simmered just beneath the surface, and increasingly strong social and labour movements were beginning to form. The full expression of these movements would surface during the 1960s and 1970s. Quebec's government experienced a "Quiet Revolution," and a whole variety of social movements emerged to demand democracy from below.

In 1982, Canada introduced a *Charter of Rights and Freedoms*. The Charter has been used to challenge discrimination and some

Abortion for
Women Caravan
Tour, Calgary,
Alberta, 1970

types of legal inequality, but it has not proven to be a panacea. It was not until 2004 that same-sex marriage was made legal in Canada. Sometimes, formal legal equality has proved not all it was cracked up to be. By almost all available social and economic measures women still lag behind men. Policies that might seriously address women's inequality, such as a national childcare program, have been dropped from the agenda of the federal government. Recent studies show that race shapes how people fare in the job force, no matter how long they and their families have lived on Canadian soil. As the case of Indigenous people makes clear, promises of formal equality mean very little when you don't have clean water to drink.

In the recent past, social movements have offered to Canada a vision of a broader and more inclusive democracy, with a global vision for equality. In 1997, many students and activists protested the Asian-Pacific Economic Co-operation Conference held in Vancouver, putting human rights and environmental concerns on the public agenda. In 2001, over 60,000 people took part in major protests in Quebec City against the Summit of the Americas and its plans for trade liberalization. In 2003, hundreds of thousands of protesters in cities across Canada joined millions from around the world in denouncing the looming war in Iraq. In 2010, nearly 20,000 people marched in Toronto against the meetings of the G20/G8. In 2011, Canadians joined the Occupy movement, confronting the power of financial institutions and unresponsive governments.

What all of these movements have in common is a profound belief that the global economic and political order is unjust, that it unfairly impoverishes nations of the global south, and that meaningful democracy requires a redistribution of wealth and the empowerment of local communities.

Arts and Culture in Canada

Culture is political. It has been a mechanism of colonialism and assimilation, as when Indigenous ceremonies like the potlatch or Sun-dance were banned in the 1880s or when French-Canadians in the western provinces were compelled to teach their children in English in the 1930s. Since the development of an official state policy of multiculturalism in 1971, arts and culture have often been seen as one of the few acceptable spaces for diverse peoples to practice "their" cultures in forums like Winnipeg's

Canadian Caribbean Association, Calgary branch, Calgary, Alberta, ca. April–May 1973

Folklorama or Toronto's annual Caribana parade. Critics of multiculturalism charge that this works to contain diversity, offering the mainstream opportunities to consume "ethnic" performance, dancing, and food, neatly packaged to charm, entertain, and never challenge. Others point out that these events, organizations, and practices provide a viable way of sustaining alternative identities and practices.

Literature has spoken powerfully to alternative visions of Canada and what it might be. In the 1960s Quebec experienced a cultural renaissance, as new forms of novels, plays, cinema, and theatre emerged. Playwright Michel Tremblay's *Les belles-soeurs* caused a sensation when it opened in 1968 for being written entirely in *joual*—colloquial street French—and bringing the experiences of working-class francophone women to the stage. In English-Canada, authors like Margaret Atwood and Alice Munro helped articulate new ideas about modern Canada and women's place in it, and are continuing to do so. In recent years, Indigenous writers Tomson Highway, Eden Robinson, and Thomas King have provided powerful statements on Canada, its land, and stories we tell about them. Authors like Michael Ondaatje, Shani Mootoo, Madeleine Thein, Dionne Brand, and Dany Laferriere grapple

Ethnic food fair, Al Azhar Temple, Calgary, Alberta, April 1956

with the reverberations of global change and migration, of what it means to move between different national contexts. Books by authors like Wayson Choy, Joy Kogawa, and Lawrence Hill reckon directly with Canadian and global histories, providing moving and sometimes searing insight on our past.

Zeitgeist Media Festival, Vancouver Art Gallery, 2011

Singer-songwriters such as Joni Mitchell, Leonard Cohen, and Buffy Sainte-Marie reflected and helped make the cultural revolution of the past forty years. Since the late 1970s, punk rockers like Vancouver's DOA have offered a loud and articulate critique of capitalism. In present day Winnipeg, hip-hop is a thriving genre with particular purchase for Indigenous artists like Wab Kinew. The ubiquity of Somali-Canadian hip-hop artist K'nann's "Wavin Flag" and the critical acclaim of Montreal's The Arcade Fire are recent reminders of the durability and influence of Canadian popular culture.

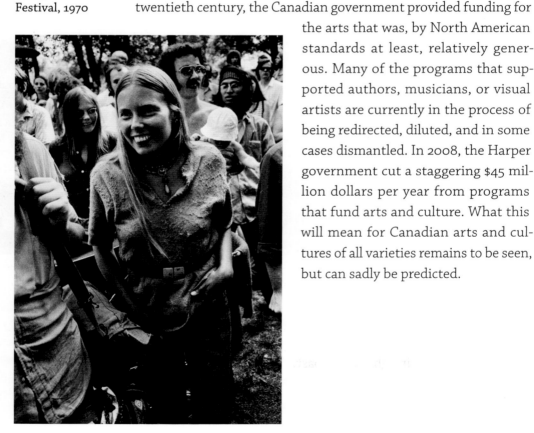

Joni Mitchell, Mariposa Folk Festival, 1970

Cultural expression needs to be nurtured. For much of the twentieth century, the Canadian government provided funding for the arts that was, by North American standards at least, relatively generous. Many of the programs that supported authors, musicians, or visual artists are currently in the process of being redirected, diluted, and in some cases dismantled. In 2008, the Harper government cut a staggering $45 million dollars per year from programs that fund arts and culture. What this will mean for Canadian arts and cultures of all varieties remains to be seen, but can sadly be predicted.

How We Govern Ourselves

We are told that Canada is a democracy, and certainly ordinary people have more say in political life here than in many countries. Yet, the Canadian political system is a very limited form of democracy, if by democracy we mean "rule by the people." Do we truly govern ourselves?

Since the 1970s, fewer and fewer Canadians choose to vote in elections. This is especially true among Canadians under the age of thirty. You must apply to become a Canadian "citizen" to vote in any election in Canada. This means waiting several years after arriving in Canada to become eligible, paying a significant application fee per person, passing a written exam in French or English, and swearing allegiance—perhaps in front of a military official—to the British Queen, who leads a Christian church. For many people, this process is a barrier to exercising their democratic rights.

Thousands of men and women are disenfranchised in Canada today, even though they contribute to society. Although we have a more inclusive democracy than we did one hundred years ago, many people remain on the sidelines.

Our parliamentary system also gives the prime minister a lot of unchecked power. It is very difficult to challenge the decisions of the majority governing party in the House of Commons. Elected

A little girl awaits her mother who is voting in civic elections, Calgary, Alberta, October 1974

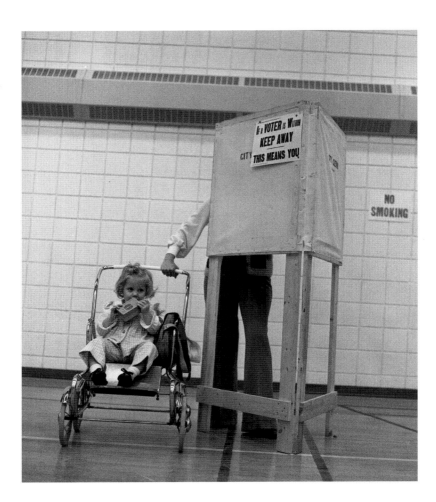

representatives almost always vote with their party, even if they do not agree with its policies. There is a Senate, but it has rarely acted against the wishes of the government of the day.

Our political system was designed by a few powerful people to serve their own interests. Canada's first prime minister, the Conservative John A. Macdonald, noted that democracy meant rule by the majority and the protection of the rights of the minority. But he opposed the universal franchise, and went on to say that the rich would always be a minority. Therefore, he supported a non-elected Senate to protect the rich from the rest of Canadians.

Belief in a more full democracy comes from the many people who have struggled to gain the right to vote, to eliminate discrimination by race or sex, to oppose the colonization of Indigenous peoples and lands, and to make Canadian laws more fair and just.

Cartoon on women's suffrage, July 8, 1914

In fact, without those movements, we might be where we were when Canada became a country in 1867: a land where Aboriginal people were considered primitive and not capable to be citizens; where women and most working people could not vote or run for office; where poverty was considered a moral failing and work-

THE VOTE GIRL

I WANT THE VOTE, AND I MEAN TO HAVE THE VOTE, THATS THE SORT OF GIRL I AM

ers had no right to organize for better wages or economic security: a country that did not trust its own people to rule themselves and failed to defend individual freedoms.

Change happened because people who desired greater individual freedom and social equality believed in the transformative potential of politics, in the broadest sense of the word. In the years following World War II, there was a heightened sense of optimism that government mattered to our daily lives and could be used as a tool for good. During a time of economic growth and policies that reduced inequality between the rich and the poor, many ordinary people made important gains in their standard of living. They tended to support social programs, such as Medicare (which was

introduced across the country in the late 1960s), that benefited them. They voted for political parties that supported greater social inclusion through the tools of activist government. Voter turnout was the highest in Canadian history.

Public debate and engagement in the workings of government demonstrated that Canadians had a lot invested in democracy. When the federal government appointed a Royal Commission on the Status of Women in 1967, thousands of Canadian women met in church basements, and wrote letters and briefs. Women and men debated its findings, and criticized the report's shortcomings. The report itself helped to mobilize women into a social movement. Today, it is hard to imagine any government report reaching into the lives of ordinary people in this way.

First Nations of Alberta Treaty members stage quiet protest, Calgary, Alberta, August 1974

The electoral participation of First Nations is a good example of the deep problems facing Canada's democracy. When they finally won the vote in 1960, First Nations people embraced this right and the majority of them voted. This sense of citizenship and inclusion

did not last. In Manitoba, voter turnout among First Nations has consistently declined from over 60 percent in the early 1960s, to below 30 percent today. This speaks to a deep sense of disenfranchisement and abandonment by government.

A crush of voters at the Altadore School polling station on civic election day, Calgary, Alberta, October 14, 1953

The very idea of active government, fair government, and responsive government has been undermined by our current political culture. Elected politicians at all levels have largely ignored the problem of a withering democracy. It is treated as a technical issue. If only we could vote online, that would do the trick. If we had a different way of running elections, like more advance polls, it would be fixed. Sometimes we discuss electing members of the federal Senate, instead of appointing them. This is like changing a light bulb when the power grid is down.

The lack of transparency and access to information about government; growing restrictions on our freedom to speak publicly, to dissent, protest, and organize collectively; and the marginalization of demands for public investment in social equality: these things will undermine the strength of our democracy—until Canadians demand the right to live otherwise.

The Justice System

Despite a strong professed commitment to the "rule of law" (the idea that laws are objective and neutral, that no one is above the law, and that the law applies equally to everyone), injustice and inequality persist in Canada.

Crime rates have been falling in recent years, yet Canada has one of the highest rates of incarceration among comparable countries. Indigenous people are grossly overrepresented in Canadian prisons, as are members of other racialized groups. Indigenous young people in many parts of the country are more likely to go to prison than to graduate from high school, let alone go to university.

People protesting the G20 summit and Toronto Police, June 2010

Female cell, police
jail, Calgary,
Alberta, 1950s

In recent years, Canada has taken an increasingly punitive approach to addressing crime and social problems, despite overwhelming research that it does not work to keep communities safer.

A young man is arrested by police in Edmonton, Alberta.

Brave individuals and groups, usually those who have felt the sting of injustice and inequality, have fought hard for changes to Canadian laws and continue to seek justice through protest, through lobbying for legislative and social change, and through legal challenges in court.

In 1982, Canada adopted the *Canadian Charter of Rights and Freedoms*, which guarantees certain rights including freedom of expression, equality, and the presumption of innocence. However, despite some significant Charter decisions (such as restrictive abortion laws being struck down in 1988), many rights are interpreted restrictively or are, in practice, ineffective at addressing deep inequality and abuses of power. In 2010, over a thousand people in Toronto were arrested and held in jail, the vast majority without charge, for participating in largely peaceful protests against government policies.

The issues that many Canadians see as violations of very basic human rights—the lack of safe drinking water in over a hundred First Nations communities and millions of Canadians living in poverty—have not been recognized as such by the courts. The Charter has been used by corporations to defend "rights" to advertise tobacco, but has not stopped the racial profiling undertaken every day by police forces across the country.

Rights without redress or enforcement are meaningless. A program that used to fund a small number of Charter court challenges was abolished by the federal government in 2006. Federal and provincial government support for publicly funded legal services ("legal aid") has diminished in recent years, meaning that many people are unrepresented by lawyers in important legal matters such as family law disputes and when facing some criminal charges.

In the face of these barriers, Canadians continue to advocate for their rights and against injustices both locally and globally, in some cases combining legal challenges with other activist strategies.

Canadian Symbols

The Chinese Restaurant

It is hard to find a Canadian town without one. After the railway was completed in the early twentieth century, the restaurant or

service industry provided employment to well over 50% of the Chinese population in some parts of the country. Either abandoned when their railway construction projects ended, or moving, as immigrants do, in search of employment opportunities, Chinese people dispersed to small towns and big cities all over the country.

Author Lily Cho calls the Chinese restaurant a place that produces "Chineseness," "Canadianness," small-town Canadian culture, and diasporic culture, all on one menu. Occasionally, such businesses were the target of anti-Asian racism, such as the well-known riot in Vancouver in 1907 when 10,000 marched through Chinatown vandalizing. But the Chinese restaurant survived. The menu itself is a tangible illustration of the complicated relationships between Chinese immigrants and their often reluctant "hosts." Usually divided into two sections, "Chinese Food" and "Canadian

8th Avenue SE, downtown Calgary, Alberta, 1973

food," the Chinese restaurant has done what few others have been capable of: it has named Canadian cuisine for Canadians. Sweet and sour pork with French fries, anyone?

Inuksuk

Maybe you've seen one driving along the Trans-Canada Highway. Or perhaps you've watched the Heritage Minute on television. Wherever it is you've come across the precarious stack of stones, the inuksuk is instantly recognizable. With deep roots in Inuit culture, the inuksuk has functioned for centuries as a marker of travel routes, fishing spots, camps, and hunting grounds. Like so much else about First Nations cultures, the inuksuk has also been easily appropriated. In 2010, Vancouver made the inuksuk its logo for the Winter Olympics and beamed it around the world for millions to see. First Nations activists complained the logo looked more like Pac-Man than an authentic inuksuk, while other native leaders heralded it as a fitting tribute to Canada's indigenous peoples. The government of Canada has gotten in on the action, building inuksuit in other countries as diplomatic gifts, most recently in Mexico, a joint venture with the Canadian Chamber of Commerce. Enukso Point, Baffin Island, home to over 100 inuksuit, has been declared a National Historic Site.

Meanwhile, the Inuit struggle to maintain control over their symbol, be it with Nunavut's flag or "Inuksuk High School" in Iqaluit. It's a constant battle. In 2007, Schomberg, Ontario, unveiled its Guinness record-breaking inuksuk, taking its place next to Sudbury's Big Nickel, Glendon's Giant Pyrogy, Shediac's Largest Lobster, and other stops along Canada's wacky tourist highways.

Niagara Falls

Niagara Falls has many lives. It has morphed from elite tourist resort to must-see stop on the European Grand Tour of North America, to working-class holiday day-trippers picnic spot, to honeymoon haven, to casino resort, and more. It has been a place where visiting Europeans gathered breathlessly to catch sight of their "first Indian," and where gay people from Walt Whitman's time on have snuck in to make snide remarks about the flagrant, rampant heterosexuality of the honeymooners. But whether people laugh at it or play with it or sermonize about it or paint it or colonize it or make electricity from it, everyone agrees on one thing: 'our' waterfall—the curvaceous Horseshoe, is nicer.

The Community Rink

The Montreal Forum and Toronto's Maple Leaf Gardens may loom large in the national imagination, but the real backbone of countless communities across Canada is the local rink. A vital social centre, the community rink doubles as concert venue, polling station, and public health clinic. Still, the rink's closest association is with hockey. So strong is the link between hockey rink and Canada that online guides to help immigrants pass their citizenship test ask the practice question: What is the significance of hockey? The answer—that it's the most popular spectator sport in Canada—may be true, but this hardly captures the rink's role in Canadian culture.

In 1956, Abby Hoffman, a nine-year-old girl, garnered international attention when she challenged the boys-only policy of minor hockey in Canada. Hoffman had played a whole season with the St. Catharines Tee Pees by suiting up at home and keeping her hair

cut short before being discovered and barred from boys' hockey. Hoffman lost that early challenge, but won many others for women's sport, eventually being made an officer of the Order of Canada and inducted into Canada's Sports Hall of Fame.

Municipal rink, Claresholm, Alberta, ca. 1900–1919

In his book *Playing Left Wing*, Yves Engler, who grew up playing hockey in Vancouver, charts his journey "from rink rat to student radical," reading hockey as a parable for progressive politics and an alternative to the game of money making.

"American Woman"

Canada's greatest rock song? Or a shining example of Canadian nationalism at its passive-aggressive—no to mention sexist—worst? Released in 1970 by Winnipeg's Guess Who, "American Woman" premiered in a curling rink in Kitchener, Ontario, and promptly topped the charts in Canada and the U.S. Nationalist anthems don't exactly promote self-reflection. And it was the (long)

American woman stay away from me
American Woman mama let me be
Don't come Hanging around my door
I don't want to see your face no more
I got more important things to do
Than spend my time growing old with you
American Woman get away from me
American woman mama let me be
Don't come knocking around my door
I don't want to see your shadow no more
Colored lights can hypnotize
Go and sparkle someone else's eyes
Now woman I said get away
American Woman listen what I say
American Woman I said get away
American woman listen what I say
Don't come hanging around my door
I don't want to see your face no more
I don't need your war machines
I don't need your ghetto scenes
Colored lights can hypnotize
Sparkle someone else's eyes
Now woman, get away from me

American woman, mama let me be
Go, gotta get away
Gotta get away
Now go go go
Gonna leave you, woman
gonna leave you, woman
Bye-bye
Bye-bye
Bye-bye
Bye-bye
You're no good for me
I'm no good for you
Gonna look you right in the eye.
Tell you what I'm gonna do
You know I'm gonna leave
You know I'm gonna go
You know I'm gonna leave
You know I'm gonna go, woman
I'm gonna leave, woman
Goodbye, American Woman

"American Woman" written by Burton Cummings,
Randy Bachman, Gary Peterson, and Jim Kale, 1970.

1960s. But this is great music to deflect by, ignoring Canada's own "ghetto scenes" and "war machines." We're good at that.

Poutine

What's brown and white and greasy all over? Poutine, of course, the latest contender for title of Canada's national food. Its origins date back to the late-1950s, in the dairy-producing region of Quebec's eastern townships where squeaky-fresh cheese curds met hot-out-of-the-fryer french fries all smothered in gravy, or "la sauce," as it's known by locals. Solidly rural and French, poutine was for a long time unknown among English-speakers

But poutine has since melted ethnic barriers and blurred class lines. In Montréal's Little Italy, mozzarella and marinara sauce replace cheese curds and gravy. The once humble becomes haute poutine with the addition of a little foie gras. In the Maritimes, lobster poutine gives the classic lobster roll a run for the tourist dollar, while out West braised Alberta beef helps the whole gloppy mess go down in a region not usually all that receptive to anything Quebecois.

Poutine

And Canadians from all parts of the country could get behind our national sport— poking fun at Americans—and laugh when comedian Rick Mercer got George W. Bush to say in complete seriousness that he was pleased to be endorsed by Prime Minister "Jean Poutine." Still, in classic Canadian fashion, we didn't really embrace poutine as a nation until it was validated by our international betters, after it became suitable to serve up on Canada Day in London's Trafalgar Square and the *New York Times* devoted a bemused feature to Quebec's "embarrassing but adored" staple.

If Canada is a sometimes fractious mix of linguistic, cultural, and regional divisions, marked by a lingering colonial complex, then poutine seems an apt symbol. In one of its creation myths, the dish's name is said to derive from a rural Quebec man who looked at the unctuous mélange and pronounced it "une maudite poutine"—a damn mess.

Canada's Economy

The Canadian Economy

Canada has a capitalist economy, which means that the bulk of the economic decisions are made by private, for-profit firms hiring wage labour. Investment, growth, and employment in capitalist economies depends on the continued profitability of private firms, giving them and their owners considerable leverage in formulating economic policy.

Yet, there is a tremendous variation between capitalist countries. Social democratic countries like Sweden use the government

Rally at Ottawa's Parliament Hill over job losses.

TABLE 1: *Gini Coefficient: After Tax Income*

	Mid 1980s	Mid 2000s
Canada	0.29	0.32
U.S.	0.34	0.37
Sweden	0.20	0.24

Source: OECD StatExtracts: Income Distribution—Inequality
http://stats.oecd.org/Index.aspx?DataSetCode=INEQUALITY

to address many of the inequalities that result from the capitalist system through programs to alleviate poverty, provide full employment, favour unions, and create relatively generous universal government programs (such as child care, education, and health care). Liberal nations (such as the U.S.) are the mirror image. These tilt the labour market and tax system in favour of business and against labour. Canada is a liberal nation, although not quite as far to the liberal end of the spectrum as the U.S.

The Canadian economy is an unequal one. Canada has a much higher level of income inequality than Sweden. Supporters of liberal economic policy in Canada argue that reducing inequality in the manner of social democratic countries would result in a less competitive country and slow economic growth. Much evidence indicates that the level of income inequality has no effect on most measures of economic health. Perhaps Canada could have a more equal economy and a stronger one.

Since the 1980s Canada has become more liberal and less equal. Its tax system is less progressive. Many of its social programs like welfare and Employment Insurance have become less generous. For example, in 1991 a couple with two children received $23,700 a year on welfare in Alberta. By 2005 that had fallen to the equivalent

TABLE 2: Median After Tax Income by Decile: Canada—families raising children		
	Late 1970s	Mid 2000s
Top 10%	108,000	131,000
20–30%	38,000	37,000
10–20%	29,000	29,000
Bottom 10%	16,000	17,000

Source: A. Yalnizyan, The Rich and the Rest of Us (Ottawa, Canadian Centre for Policy Alternatives, 2007) 25

of $19,500. Unionization rates have fallen and workers in Canada have faced increasing competition from workers elsewhere. The result has been stagnant wages for many Canadian workers. The real incomes of the bottom 30% of families in Canada are either pretty much the same or actually lower in the mid-2000s than they were in the mid-1970s, while the income of the richest 10% of the population has increased by $23,000 over the same period. To make matters worse, families in the bottom 30% are working longer hours than they were a generation ago. The share of profits earned by firms in the Canadian economy has increased from 25% in the early 1980s to 33% in 2005.

The benefits of Canada's liberal economy go to those at the top end of the income spectrum, while many average working Canadians are actually worse off than they were a generation ago. While some say that this is inevitable, examples like Sweden show us that a more egalitarian economy, in which economic benefits are much more broadly shared, is possible.

Canada's Regions

C anada is large and spread out. It borders the Pacific Ocean to the west, the Atlantic Ocean to the east, and the Arctic Ocean to the north, and is connected to Asia, Europe, and the circumpolar north. Today, most Canadians live near the Canada-United States border to the south. This border cuts through Indigenous territories and has long been challenged by Indigenous peoples, including those of the Six Nation Iroquois Confederacy.

The U.S. is powerful, wealthy, and populous country, and it is difficult for Canada to live beside it and not be overwhelmed by it. The Free Trade Agreement signed between Canada and the U.S. in 1988 and the North American Free Trade Agreement signed between Canada, Mexico, and the U.S. in 1994 eliminated some key barriers between the countries involved. American television, products, and ideas flow freely into Canada, but only occasionally in the opposite direction. Following 9/11, Canada has brought its immigration and border-control practices into closer line with those of the U.S.

In some ways, the border matters more and more. As of June 2009, Canadian citizens need a passport to enter the United States. It is harder and harder for peoples to cross the border into Canada. Canada grants residency to about 20,000 immigrants each year, but many others are turned away or enter without legal status. About

A man stands in protest on Parliament hill in Ottawa, February 26, 2011

1.5% of the population in Canada is not authorized or documented, and these people find it difficult or impossible to claim basic rights and benefits. Approximately 8,000 people are deported from Canada every year. Across Canada, groups like "No One is Illegal/Personne n'est illegal" work to assist migrants, question a system that calls some people illegal, and help us imagine a world without borders.

The National Capital

Queen Victoria made Ottawa the capital of Canada in 1857. Before the Queen of England chose this small lumber town, a number of places, including Kingston, Ontario, have claimed to be the capital. In Canada, nothing is certain, and everything is up for debate.

Provinces and Territories

Canada has ten provinces and three territories. Provinces have the powers of self-government, or the right to elect their own governments. Territories do not, and are governed only with the approval of Ottawa, much how England used to govern Canada.

Population

Canada has a population of about 34 million people. For many Canadians, local, regional, or other national identities are more important than or as important as national ones. People might identify with their country of origin, or with the Indigenous nations they hail from, or with the nation of Quebec. The Haudenosaunee carry their own passports as a powerful sign of the belief in the sovereignty of their Indigenous nation. In 2007, a poll found that only 38% of Canadians identified first and foremost with the nation of Canada. Almost one in four said they identified first with their province or region. This is especially true in Quebec, where forty-two percent of people identified with Quebec before Canada. It was only in Ontario that the majority of people identified primarily with the nation of Canada.

The Atlantic Provinces

The Atlantic region has been historically, and some would say systemically, economically underdeveloped. The region's resource economies continue to struggle and sway depending on global demand. Unemployment is higher than the national average, and the region receives fewer new migrants than many other parts of the country. Yet people's fierce loyalty to the places that make up Atlantic Canada persists.

Newfoundland and Labrador

Newfoundland did not join Canada as a province until 1949. It retains a sense of separation and distinctiveness, symbolized by its own time zone set one half-hour apart. This province includes the Island

of Newfoundland and the adjacent mainland territory of Labrador. Newfoundland's population is made up mostly of settlers, many of whom hail from families who migrated in the 1700 and 1800s. Labrador is a largely Indigenous society. The economy has not recovered from the devastation of the cod-fishery in the late twentieth century. In 2006, Newfoundland and Labrador's unemployment rate was 18.6%, nearly three times the national average.

Stamp from the Dominion of Newfoundland, ca. 1935

Prince Edward Island

Prince Edward Island (P.E.I.) is the smallest province. In the nineteenth century, Islanders successfully challenged the semi-feudal system of land owning that kept them from owning their own farms. P.E.I. was the site of the first meetings to negotiate Canadian confederation, and this much-celebrated tie to the federal nation-state must sometimes seem hollow in a province with a relatively small population and high unemployment rates. One of the Island's most famous products is Lucy Maud Montgomery's *Anne of Green Gables*, a novel that provides an excellent example of the complexities of early twentieth-century feminist thought in Canada.

Nova Scotia

Nova Scotia has the highest population and the lowest unemployment rate of the Atlantic Provinces. In the 1600s, Nova Scotia was settled by French settlers. In the 1750s, the Acadians were deported by Britain, and their lands appropriated, just as the Indigenous Mi'kmaq had been before them. In the late 1700s Nova Scotia became home to a vibrant community of free Black people, one that would continue to struggle for equality, recognition, and sometimes survival. In the 1940s, hairdresser Viola Desmond challenged the legality of racial segregation. Twenty years later, the historic Black community of Africville was razed as part of an urban renewal movement that had no room for it. It is this rich and complicated history that plays a key part in what poet George Elliot Clark calls the "Africadia."

Gay Pride Parade, Halifax, Nova Scotia, 2010

New Brunswick

New Brunswick is home to the second largest proportion of French-speakers in Canada. The province relies heavily on the primary industries of forestry, agriculture, and fishing. The power of a few capitalists looms large over the province's economy. The Irving empire is valued at approximately $7–9 billion (U.S.), is the single biggest landowner in New Brunswick, and the owner of all but one of New Brunswick's daily newspapers. The french fry empire of the McCain family is based in Florenceville, and is Canada's second largest private company. Given the extent to which a small number of wealthy individuals dominate New Brunswick's economy, it is no surprise that the province's politics tend to be conservative, occasionally flipping back and forth between Liberals and Progressive Conservatives, both equally committed to keeping big business happy.

Central Canada

There is no one "Central Canada." There are provinces of Quebec and Ontario, the most recent iteration of a long, complicated, and not always successful attempt to divide the sphere of mainly English-speaking from mainly French-speaking Canada.

Quebec

Quebec flag and map

Modern Quebec traces its roots to New France. Now, nearly eight million people live there, and more than three-quarters are primarily French-speaking. Contemporary Quebecois have worked to preserve the unique, French-speaking culture within a mostly English-speaking continent and within a nation where they make up a smaller and smaller part of the overall population. By trying to wrest economic and cultural control from an English-speaking elite and make the Quebecois "maître chez nous" in the 1960s, and supporting nationalist political parties like the Parti Québécois, they have worked to nurture and advance French Canadian culture. In 2006, about nine percent of Quebecois were members of a "visible minority," most of them living around the city of Montreal. Newcomers to Quebec are more likely to be unemployed than elsewhere in the country. In 2007, the provincial government empowered a two-man team to investigate the question of "reasonable accommodation," or how and to what extent newcomers should be accommodated within Quebec. What these changes will mean for Quebec has yet to be fully seen.

Ontario

With almost 40% of the nation's population and the bulk of the country's manufacturing industry, Ontario is the wealthiest and most populous province in Canada. Manufacturing made the province wealthy throughout most of the twentieth century, but has made it vulnerable to the collapse of the American stock market and economy that began in 2007. Ontario, and especially its major

Jack Layton Memorial, Toronto City Hall, August 2011

city of Toronto, is where many newly arrived people in Canada have chosen to live, especially since the 1950s. Torontonians' oft-made claim to be the "most multicultural city in the world" is both wrong and impossible to quantify, but the city is marked by a genuine diversity that has changed the course of the city and the country's history. In 2006, almost half or 46% of people in Toronto were born outside of Canada. If "old Ontario" ever really existed, Toronto shows that it does not now.

The Prairie Provinces

Most of Alberta, Saskatchewan, and Manitoba are not technically prairies, and the provinces have many differences, including some staggering political ones. These three provinces do share a relatively late history of colonization, a significant Aboriginal population, and a dependence on a volatile world market for staple agricultural products, especially grain.

Manitoba

North American Indigenous Games, 2002, Winnipeg, Manitoba

The province of Manitoba was born out of the post-colonial struggles of Métis leader Louis Riel. After the *Manitoba Act* of 1870, the population gradually became less Indigenous and more and more dominated by settlers. Settler migration was facilitated by the federal government, which wished to disperse the Indigenous people, settle their claims to the land with treaties, and relocate them onto reserves. During the late nineteenth and twentieth century, Manitoba developed

Winnipeg General Strike, Winnipeg, June 21, 1919

a significant financial, distribution and manufacturing economy and a population drawn from all over Europe and North America. Manitoba was the first province to grant most women the right to vote in 1916. The "prairie metropolis" of Winnipeg was the location for the continent's most spectacular and sustained general strike in 1919. Like Saskatchewan, Manitoba has a tradition since the 1970s of periodically electing social-democratic provincial governments.

Saskatchewan

The provinces of Saskatchewan and Alberta were created out of the Northwest territories in 1905, examples of the federal government's vision for an agricultural, settler west. In the late nineteenth and early twentieth century, Saskatchewan became the province most closely associated with stock images of what "prairie" was: dependent on agriculture, especially wheat; disproportionately rural; vulnerable to an unforgiving environment and fluctuating world economy. This was an economy that Indigenous peoples were largely excluded from, and the costs of this become clearer as the population of Saskatchewan becomes increasingly an Indigenous one. As in Manitoba, about 15% of the province of Saskatchewan is Aboriginal, and it is a young and growing population.

Environment Minister Ralph Klein facing pulp mill objectors, Alberta, ca. October–December, 1989

Alberta

In contemporary Canadian popular discourse, Alberta is famed for its conservatism and the wealth the oil industry has brought. For much of the twentieth century, Alberta was better known for its social radicalism.

Alberta nurtured the feminism and social politics of suffragist, author and politician Nellie McClung and the feminism and racism of judge and author Emily Murphy. The first women elected to provincial governments were elected in Alberta in 1917. Social and fiscal conservatism may have dominated Alberta's politics for the last half of the twentieth century, but the 2010 election of Naheed Nenshi, a left-leaning, Harvard-educated policy-wonk and the first Muslim mayor a major Canadian city, suggests that the province might be returning to some of its other histories.

Police attempting to contain demonstration of Calgary Coalition against War and Poverty, Calgary, Alberta, 2004

The West Coast

The West Coast presumably means the province of British Columbia, which includes the west coast of northern North America. Cheap comments about the province's physical beauty detract from the area's complicated history and present. British Columbia may be a place of beauty, but it is also a place of longstanding conflict about who can live there and under what terms, who owns the land, and how people should live on it or by it.

British Columbia

This territory was first colonized in the middle years of the 1800s, when Britain established the colonies of Vancouver Island and then British Columbia. In British Columbia, Indigenous claims to the land were not usually settled by treaty, and as a result almost all of British Columbia's lands are currently contested by Indigenous nations who claim ownership of the land. Patterns of trade, migration, and communication have long tied the west coast to the American territories to south, and to Asia. British Columbia's Asian population is as old as any other non-Indigenous population. In 2009, 24.6% of people in British Columbia were identified as "visible minorities," the largest percentage in Canada.

Hockey fans and a historic mural, Vancouver, B.C., 2011.

The Northern Territories

The Yukon Territory, the Northwest Territories, and Nunavut are Canada's northernmost jurisdictions. Each is governed as "territories" rather than provinces.

Yukon

The Indigenous territories around the Yukon River came into intensive contact with non-Indigenous peoples during the gold rush of 1898. The Territory has two cities, Whitehorse and Dawson City, and is the only one of the three territories where non-Indigenous people outnumber Indigenous ones. It has also been the most successful negotiating some of the key kinds of self-government that southerners take for granted. This includes dropping the word "territory" from its official name.

The Northwest Territories

The "Northwest Territories" were created in 1870 when the Hudson's Bay Company "transferred" a substantial part of northern North

Industrial truck on the Dempster Highway, Northwest Territories

America to Canada, a transaction famously treated more or less like a real estate deal. Gradually, territories and provinces have been separated out, leaving the contemporary North West Territories lying between the Yukon to the west and Nunavut to the east. Over half of the population identified as Indigenous, most of them First Nations and a minority Inuit.

Nunavut

Nunavut was cleaved out of the Northwest Territories in 1999. This was in part the result of a larger struggle for Indigenous self-government and Inuit cultural autonomy. The Arctic has a long history of contact with Europeans. There are written accounts of the Arctic produced as early as 1576. Inuit people's ability to secure significant tools of self-government and highly symbolic acts of cultural transformation —including stripping the capital of a name commemorating a British explorer, Frobisher Bay, and renaming

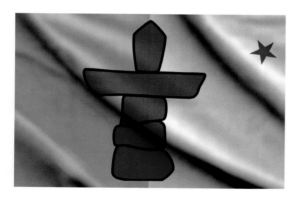

Nunavut flag

it an Inuit name, Iqaluit—is a sign that not all of Canada has been remade in the model of settler colonialism. Almost 70% of people in Nunavut report that Inuktitut is their "mother tongue."

15 or More Things to Think About....

1. Who are First Nations?

2. What is settler-colonialism and why did European Empires seek to conquest North America?

3. Who are some of the people living and working in Canada who are excluded from citizenship? How do laws make distinctions between who is a "citizen" and who is not?

4. Rebellion, civil disobedience and dissent have been crucial factors in the expansion of individual and collective rights. What were some of these challenges to state authority? How have social movements and contentious politics helped to shape citizenship rights?

5. How has Canadian immigration policy changed over the years? What different people have been denied entry to Canada, and why?

6. Who was Louis Riel?

7. Why do symbols of militarism and royalty—Mounties, soldiers, and Queens—appear in many recent representations of the Canadian nation?

8. What was the "Persons Case" and why is it important to the struggle for sex and gender equity in Canada?

9. What does the deployment of consumable items—coffee, beer, donuts and poutine—as national symbols tell us about Canadian citizenship?

10. What are some of the ways that French-speaking and English-speaking people tell different stories about Canada's history? Why are these stories different?

11. Could we have a stamp that commemorated the Northwest Rebellion, the Winnipeg General Strike, the Front de Libération du Québec, or the Abortion Caravan? Why not?

12. If Canada is a "nation of laws," protected by the *Charter of Rights and Freedoms*, why are protestors still subject to arrest without charge?

13. Paying taxes is an obligation of Canadian citizens, residents and corporations. Is the Canadian tax system fair? Do all those who are obliged to pay taxes do so equitably?

14. Look at *Discover Canada: The Rights and Responsibilities of Citizenship* (available at http://www.cic.gc.ca/english/resources/publications/discover/index.asp). Why did the current Conservative government produce the *Discover Canada* guide? What values does it promote? What symbols of Canada does it celebrate and what ones does it downplay or omit?

15. Can we create a more equitable and just version of Canadian citizenship? Or should we instead work to challenge the ideas of nations, borders, and citizenship and build global alliances?

Contributors

David Churchill is Associate Professor of U.S. history at the University of Manitoba and is the Director of the University of Manitoba Institute for the Humanities. He writes and researches the history of radical social movements and queer history. He is the coordinator of the Institute's LGBTTQ (Lesbian, Gay, Bi-Sexual, Transgendered, Two-Spirited & Queer) Oral History Initiative, documenting the lives of activists in Winnipeg.

Dominique Clément is an Assistant Professor in the Department of Sociology at the University of Alberta. He is the author of *Canada's Rights Revolution: Social Movements and Social Change, 1937-1982*. He is also the editor for *Debating Dissent: Canada and the Sixties* and *Alberta's Human Rights Story: The Search for Equality and Justice*. He manages www.HistoryOfRights.com on the history of the human rights movement in Canada.

Karen Dubinsky teaches in the departments of Global Development Studies and History at Queen's University, and writes about global child politics. Her most recent book is *Babies Without Borders: Adoption and Migration across the Americas*. In 1991, she took, and failed, the 1955 Canadian Citizenship test, which she discovered while sorting through her recently deceased immigrant grandmother's belongings.

Ian Hudson is an Associate Professor of economics at the University of Manitoba researching in political economy. His most recent book (with Robert Chernomas) is *The Gatekeeper: 60 Years of Economics According to the New York Times*. He also writes on Canadian economic issues as a research associate for the Canadian Centre for Policy Alternatives.

Esyllt Jones studies the history of health, disease, and social movements, and is an Associate Professor of History at the University of Manitoba. Author of *Influenza 1918: Disease, Death and Struggle in Winnipeg*, she is also a member of the ARP editorial collective.

Mary-Ellen Kelm teaches History at Simon Fraser University where she is the Canada Research Chair in Indigenous histories, medicine and society. Her most recent book is *A Wilder West: A History of Rodeo in Western Canada*. She is currently involved in a project to preserve the history of Alternative Vancouver, organizations and individuals who envisioned alternative living environments and education in Vancouver in the 1960s, 1970s and 1980s.

Mark Leier teaches history at Simon Fraser University. His most recent book is *Bakunin: The Creative Passion*.

Steven Maynard teaches Canadian history at Queen's University in Kingston, Ontario. He's been active in and writing about sexual politics for over twenty years. Steven lives in Toronto.

Sean Mills is the author of *The Empire Within: Postcolonial Thought and Political Activism in Sixties Montreal*. He teaches history at the University of Toronto. A historian of Quebec and Canada post-1945, his research interests include postcolonial thought, migration, race, nationalism, gender, and the history of empire and oppositional movements.

Debra Parkes is an Associate Professor in the Faculty of Law, University of Manitoba. Her research addresses the possibilities and challenges of pursuing social justice through litigation and other rights-based strategies. She is the English Language Editor of the *Canadian Journal of Women and the Law*.

Adele Perry is Associate Professor and Canada Research Chair (Tier II) in the Department of History, University of Manitoba. She is the author of *On the Edge of Empire*, a co-editor of *Rethinking Canada: The Promise of Women's History*, and is working on a book length study of an elite Creole/Métis family and circuits of migration and rule in the nineteenth-century British empire.

Credits and Permissions

INTERIOR

"Immigrants Arriving at Winnipeg Station, Manitoba, about 1909." McCord Museum MP-0000.2328.13

"Wampum String." McCord Museum M13321

"Cha Chay Pay Way Ti's Map of the Waterways of a Part of Northern Manitoba." Peter Fiddler, 1806. In John Warkentin and Richard I. Ruggles. *Manitoba Historical Atlas: a Selection of Facsimile Maps, Plans, and Sketches from 1612 to 1969.* Winnipeg: Historical and Scientific Society of Manitoba, 1969, p. 142

"Portrait of a Haitian Woman." McCord Museum M 12067

"Le Canada." Pierre du Val, 1653. In John Warkentin and Richard I. Ruggles. *Manitoba Historical Atlas: a Selection of Facsimile Maps, Plans, and Sketches from 1612 to 1969.* Winnipeg: Historical and Scientific Society of Manitoba, 1969, p. 32

"The Pallisaded Village of Lachine, 1689." McCord Museum M967.50.8

"Encampment of the Loyalists in Johnstown, a New Settlement on the Banks of the River St. Lawrence, in Canada West." Archives of Ontario, RG 2-344-0-0-89.

"The Burning of the Parliament Building in Montreal." McCord Museum M11588

"Back View of the Church of St. Eustache and Dispersion of the Insurgents." McCord Museum M4777.6

"Notice to Intending Emigrants for North America. For Sydney, Cape Briton, Pictou, Nova Scotia & Quebec, 1845." Glenbow Archives Poster-28.

"Interior of Workshop." McCord Museum M930.50.8.79"

"Louis Riel, Montreal, Quebec, 1868." Glenbow Archives NA-2631-1

"Home of Galician Settlers, Rosthern, SK, about 1910." McCord Museum MP-0000.1405.5

"Native Graveyard, Lebret, SK, 1885." Glenbow Archives NA-908-2

"Mothers' Picnic, Stanley Park, BC, 1935." Glenbow Archives NA-3634-10

"Presentation of Petition by Political Equality League for Enfranchisement of Women, Winnipeg, MB, 23 December 1915." Archives of Manitoba, Still Images Section, Events Collection, 173/3

"The Komagata Maru in Vancouver's Port, July 1914." City of Vancouver Archives, 7-123, James Luke Quiney Fonds

"Some of the First Cree Enlistees, The Pas, 1914." Archives of Manitoba, Still Images Section, John A. Campbell Collection-Series IV, 1

"Internment Camp At Banff, Alberta, c 1914-1918." Glenbow Archives NA-2126-18

"Waving goodbye to Japanese Canadians being sent to a work camp near Jasper, Alberta in February 1942." City of Vancouver Archives, City of Vancouver Archives, 1194-12, Jack Lindsay Photographers

"Signs from a protest against Canada's involvement in global wars." Sergei Bachlakov/Shutterstock.com Image ID: 11965399

"Inspired by the Indians of All Tribes Occupation of Alcatraz (1969-71), members of the Akwesasne Mohawk Warrior Society Reclaim Look Island, near Cornwall, Ontario, 1970." In Gerry Kopelow, *All Our Changes: Images From the Sixties Generation.* Winnipeg: University of Manitoba Press, 2009

"Anti-war Protests on 8th Avenue [Stephen Avenue], Calgary, AB, 1971." Glenbow Archives NA-2864-19095

"New Canadians Learning English, Calgary, AB, 1977." Glenbow Archives NA-2864-29724

"North End Winnipeg, Manitoba, ca. 1979." In John Paskievich, *The North End.* Winnipeg: University of Manitoba Press, 2007

"Abortion for Women Caravan Tour, Calgary, AB, 1970." Glenbow Archives NA-2864-5986

"Canadian Caribbean Association, Calgary Branch, 1973." Glenbow Archives NA-2864-22955

"Ethnic Food Fair, Al Azhar Temple, Calgary, AB, 1956." Glenbow Archives NA-5600-7976b

"Zeitgeist Media Festival, Vancouver Art Gallery, September 2011." Denis Kuvaev/ Shutterstock.com Image ID: 84509719

"A Luminous Joni Mitchell at the Mariposa Folk Festival, 1970." In Gerry Kopelow, *All Our Changes: Images From the Sixties Generation.* Winnipeg: University of Manitoba Press, 2009

"A Little Girl Awaits Her Mother Who is Voting in Civic Elections, Calgary, AB, 1974." Glenbow Archives NA-2864-26228

"Cartoon on Women's Suffrage, 1914." Glenbow Archives NA-3818-14

"First Nations of Alberta Treaty Members Stage Quiet Protest, Calgary, AB, 1974." Glenbow Archives NA-2864-25985

"A Crush of Voters at the Altadore School Polling Station on Civic Election Day, Calgary, AB, 1953." Glenbow Archives NA-5600-6732c

"People protesting the G20 Summit and Toronto police, June 2010." arindambanerjee/Shutterstock.com Image ID: 56579431

"Female Cell, Police Jail, Calgary, AB, 1950s," Glenbow Archives NA-2861-36

"A young man is arrested by police in Edmonton, Alberta." Jack Dagley Photography/ Shutterstock.com Image ID: 7770703

"8th Avenue SE, Downtown Calgary, AB, 1973." Glenbow Archives NA5516-10b

"Municipal Rink, Claresholm, AB, ca. 1900-1919." Glenbow Archives MA-5257-50

"Poutine." Margoe Edwards/Shutterstock.com Image ID: 44362894

"Rally at Ottawa's Parliament Hill over Canadian job losses." David P. Lewis/ Shutterstock.com Image ID: 3419142

"A man stands in protest on Parliament Hill in Ottawa. In the background are the Parliament Buildings and another protest. Ottawa, February 26, 2011." Ryerson Clark/istockphoto File #: 15902282

"Stamp from the Dominion of Newfoundland, circa 1935." rook76/Shutterstock.com Image ID: 79551190.

"Gay Pride Parade, Halifax, 2010." V. J. Matthew/ Shutterstock.com Image ID: 58073275

"Quebec flag and map." Atlaspix/ Shutterstock Image ID: 72749764

"Jack Layton memorial, Toronto City Hall, August 2011." Paul McKinnon/ Shutterstock.com Image ID: 83531176

"Winnipeg General Strike, Winnipeg, 21 June 1919." Archives of Manitoba, Still Images Section, Foote Collection, 1696

"North American Indigenous Games, 2002 Winnipeg, Manitoba." Keith Levit/ Shutterstock.com Image ID: 1124435.

"Environment Minister Ralph Klein Facing Pulp Mill Objectors, Alberta, 1989." Glenbow Archives PA-1599-354c-81

"Police Attempting to Contain Demonstration of Calgary Coalition Against War and Poverty, Calgary, Alberta, June 30, 2004." Glenbow Archives M-9390-13-1

"Hockey fans and a historical mural, Vancouver 2011." Sergei Bachlakov/ Shutterstock.com Image ID: 79248544

"Industrial truck on the Dempster Highway, Northwest Territories." Oksana Perkins/ Shutterstock.com Image ID: 15753874

"Nunavut flag." Rene Grycner/Shutterstock. com Image ID: 79218805

FRONT COVER
"Occupy Toronto, October 15 2011." Paul McKinnon/Shutterstock.com Image ID: 86731732

"Skating on Ottawa's Rideau Canal." Vlad Ghiea/Shutterstock.com Image ID: 3433918

American Woman
Written by Burton Cummings, Randy Bachman, Gary Peterson and Jim Kale (c) 1970 (Renewed 1998) SHILLELAGH MUSIC (BMI)/Administered by BUG MUSIC All Rights Reserved Used by Permission *Reprinted by Permission of Hal Leonard Corporation*

Acknowledgements

THIS BOOK WAS TRULY A COLLABORATIVE PROJECT, and so there are many contributions to acknowledge. Everyone who wrote sections of the guide was a model citizen, responding to tight deadlines, submitting to editorial revisions with grace, offering feedback, and generally supporting the project in a generous spirit and with enthusiasm. We had an awesome team of smart and engaged scholars.

The project has encountered a positive response from many people, but we would like to thank in particular the support of Ian McKay and Franca Iacovetta, who were encouraging from the start. Ian's work, soon to be published in Ian McKay and Jamie Swift, Warrior Nation: Rebranding Canada in a Fearful Age (Between the Lines, 2011) has been germinal to this undertaking, and deserves special mention. Jon Malek helped us to get this project off the ground and keep us on track in the early days. The project received financial support from the University of Manitoba, and Adele Perry acknowledges the support of the Canada Research Chairs program.

Thanks to David Carr at University of Manitoba Press, whose experience with historical images helped when time was almost up. We are grateful for the introduction to photographers Gerry Kopelow and John Paskievich, who generously allowed us to include their evocative photographs in the book.

On this project, even more so than is normally the case for writers, we relied on our publisher. Richard Wood and John K. Samson, thanks for your perfect combination of calm and prompting. Terry Corrigan at Relish Design, who designed both the interior and the cover, worked patiently with us through an unconventional project, one that evolved constantly. You were all a joy to work with.

A number of people have seen and made comments on some version of this guide, which in the end is one iteration of the many possible. Despite the usual disclaimers (all mistakes and inadequacies are our own) we hope the guide is something we can all sink our teeth into. We look forward to a lot of conversations about the meaning of Canadian nationhood, borders, citizenship, rights, and equality.